SICK TRANSIT

SICK
TRANSIT

GLORIA
STRUTHERS

Illustrations by Ros Asquith

SINCLAIR-STEVENSON

First published in Great Britain by
Sinclair-Stevenson Limited
7/8 Kendrick Mews
London SW7 3HG England

13/1/93

British Library Cataloguing in Publication Data
A CIP catalogue record for this book is available from the British Library.

ISBN: 1 85619 186 9 (hardback)
ISBN: 1 85619 190 7 (paperback)

Typeset by Rowland Phototypesetting Limited,
Bury St Edmunds, Suffolk

Printed and bound in Great Britain by
Clays Ltd, St Ives plc

CONTENTS

ix

The Queen Dreams

One wants to be a TV Mum
Holding up a shirt critically
While coy children who never vomit, swear
Or suffer from childish diseases ask
What beans means,
And demand socks without blemish
While their bland background father
Dreams of Rosie, the Real Thing.
Her grimey smalls, the way she wears
Her drawers two days on the trot, slut,
And One smiles back at him
Benign behind the Weetabix.

One wants to be a female heroine
With a large Warner vision frontage
Continually falling down in situations
Of the utmost peril,
Emitting small screams
Until One's man returns to fend off
Tigers, giant lizards, or in this case,
Savage Hordes,
Later pressing One to his manly bosom
As One comes at him with nipples at maximum alert,
Mouth oozing red wet promise
As the credits rise
Over One's bustle, or in this case
The desert sands.

One wants to be nearly six foot tall,
Bronzed, elegantly emaciated,
Tawny in a tanga
For the wearing of which One is obliged
To pluck out otherwise public pubic hairs

Pacing narcissistically
On a beach
In sunglasses,
All the men going
Oh boy
When it is patently obvious
That One is in fact
A girl.

One wants to be the new Francis
Standing in the street
While all the animals run
To One,
A quality of stillness and repose
About One's holier-than-thou person,
One feeding the pigeons and murmuring
'Little brothers,'
As they crap on One's feet.

One wants to be Mother Theresa
Saving the lepers in Calcutta
Ancient, seamed and wrinkled
By One's great love,
A leathery, holy virgin embodying
In One's wizened frame
The great female virtú
Compassion: The Comprehension
Of Pain.

One wants to wear dresses with practically
No front
So that everyone says it's a miracle
How she keeps it up,
And One shall be cruel to an Onassis type
And spend all his money
On lots of frocks,

Spurning his love, humiliating
The old creep
And laughing in a hard-hearted manner
Should he go down on his knees.

One wants to be eleven years old, with Margaret Rose,
And wear socks
And Clark's sandals,
Playing hopscotch in frilly knickers
And picking the scabs off One's knees
Bashing up One's brothers if One had any
And should reckoning come
Denying it, looking frail
And threatening tears,
Later
Spitting through the gap
In One's teeth.

One wants to be – well, almost anyone really
And as they say
Rather you than One.

Fairy Story

When my Mum and Dad got married,
They lived happily ever after.

No More Lettuce

Dear John,
    Let me speak plainly.
    I think it was when he first gave me as a gift
    Gateaux. From a low position, he arose creakingly.
    His knees had seized, the synovial fluids of the patella
    Giving up the ghost. This fella, I thought,
    Is a human being;
    He is not honed to Superman proportions
    Nor is he wont, winters, to run around
    A rugby pitch, doing press-ups
    While I scrum down in Tesco's
    Foraging for fibre.

    He does not play cricket or the field (Wanda,
                                Wednesdays)
    Nor dive, all the wives of other men going
    Ooh
    I doubt he spends much time
    Flexing his pecs, going, 'Gaze woman
    And be grateful', also, 'Where is my tea? None
    For you: only slim women, aerobically trimmed
                               women
    Such as work out well o'nights
    May bed with me. Cellulite's not sweet, dear,
    Nor's rolls. What ought to be taut
    In you
    Hangs down in folds.'

    So.

    With fags forgone and booze forbid I have lived
    Bun-less in Ealing
    Mindful of yogurt, sans crisps, sans chips, no chocs

And all for frocks a size too small:
'Let her not eat cake,' you also said,
'For fear of Woman, Outsize, in bed.'
On reflection, dear John, I think you'll find
I've washed and ironed your jockstrap
For the very last time.

You get ready for the nets, pet,
This inning's up with me.

I'm eating fatty paté, John, parkin, pasta too
Bread and butter, bacon, batter-pud and choux;
Gin's stopped play, I'm happy to confide – it's all
                               hanging out now
I've nothing more to hide: his outlook, though bi-focal
Is encouragingly wide.

He's bald, I'm fat
And that, dear John,
Is that.

                                         Love,
                                         Gloria.

Aesthete's Lament

This one
Worshipped from afar
The masculine form divine
Standing revealed in monumental stone
The super-human grace
Of human perfection, statues,
Chipped at and smoothed at by inspired hands
Those Greeks, yes, even
Those Roman copy-cats,
Those masters of the Cinquecento
And others, who tore from shivering rock
Stone-cold bodies,
       Naked.
Aye, there's the rub: naked,
Stretching taut marble limbs
Each curve and muscle vibrant
With petrified life:
They forced their way
Into my consciousness.
I never could see the young man
After that
Without re-zoning him in Time and Place
As model for a master
And having erected in my head
This masterpiece,
Found he had rocks between his ears:
Brain-dead.

Flat-Mate

When I had my hair done, highlighted and streaked,
She had hers done too, and she looked
Better than me: bits of mine fell off and out, hers didn't.

When I went Green Peace and was friendly towards the Earth
She ate steak and wore wolf and looked
Better than me, foxy; I was in natural yak, eating grains.

When I slimmed and starved on two calories a day
She ate roast potatoes and saveloy and still looked
Better than me: even gaunt, I was fatter than she.

When I started aerobics and tended to sweat a lot
She lay limp on the sofa and stuffed chocs. Somehow she
                                                  looked
Better than me: I looked like Rambo, in lycra.

When I had men round to entertain
I made soufflés that sank and she made eyes at them. She
                                                  looked
Better than me: also I took her advice and wore puce.

When I finally got a fiancé, Quentin, blind as a bat and a
                                                  wimp,
She came as a bridesmaid in pink silk. She looked
Better than me: I was swathed in tulle, and looked a fool.

When I went into labour and had quads, she ran off with
                                                  Quent
Who became a big gent in the City: so I caught her, killed her,
And buried her in the cellar.
And you know what? She still looked better than me: even
                                                  as a corpse.

10

A Cavalier Approach

I learned to smash a Sierra,
Coasting on to crash into a Rolls.
Wrong. Got a slap from Ron, reeled,
Reversed over a Reliant
Then stalled at Marble Arch with a slam
To let the pigeons march past.
A jam as far as Enfield ensued.
I over-steered at Paddington to escape,
Straight onto the Paris-bound freight crate.
What was so wrong, why was he appalled
At channelling a level-crossing
Locomotively
Via Vauxhall?

I file heretoforthwith instanter
For divorce: custody
Of course of the cats, me,
The goldfish, the one that's left, he.
I go for the split:
Pierre's french engine is more elastic
With EEC advantage to it and not plastic.
It's vehicularly expeditious, too,
For when I grasp his gear-stick,
I get instructions repetitious
In double de-clutch
Yoo-hoo.

So what the L ?
As into his arms I fall
I reckon a Deux Chevaux is better
Than no vorsprung durch technickers at all.

Hello Hans.

Stepping Out

I read your letter, in his coat,
How he made a woman of you
You love him so, you wrote.
I expect he loves you too, why not?
I saw you once.
I was in the supermarket, worn out
With pushing the pram, managing the other two
And negotiating the shopping queue.
You were fresh and neat, high-styled,
Dangling your chic little purchases from the boutique,
Your high heels tapping cheerily
On the pavement. You're lithe,
Whereas I've been brought to bed
Just one too many times for beauty's sake.
I used to work, like you, once,
But I gave it up. For some years now
All the working knowledge I've had's been of him,
His laundry, his little whims and habits
I won't say what, you'll find out soon
Because I'm going now,
Leaving it all to you.
You want to be by his side, dear?
You want to take my place?
Well, why not? It's natural, but I want to go with grace.

I'll have to leave the kids.
I can't support them, he'll understand.
Graham likes to keep the purse strings
In his own very careful hands,
So I'm dropping them at your flat, dear,
You'll have to get their tea: careful
How you boil Gray's egg in the morning,
And his collars, keep them pressed.

I've stocked the freezer; I've left
A list of useful numbers
Doctors, plumbers and the vet's
So Graham doesn't get depressed
By domestic detail: you'll have to see to them.
Dust carefully; his mother
Drops by to spy on impulse. She's got a parental eye
For the dereliction of her boy and his children.
She's an old cow, by the bye, but she comes as part of the
                                                    deal
Of lousy cards I now leave to you. The kids?
Miss them? Not much. They're a precocious brood,
Tristram, Iphigenia and Gavin (his choice)
All spavined, like their Dad.

I'm glad, sadly, in a way, to go
And leave them all to you
But I'm sure that you're deserving
And what else can I do?
You're not the first, dear,
But by golly, you'll be the last.
He made a woman out of you, did he?
But just look what he did to me.

No looking back: I'll get my hat.
Not raging into that dark night I'll go,
But gently hopeful, mildly yearning –
Because I'll miss the cat.

Fat Chance

She dreamed a dream
Of a fat man,
Flesh feverishly straining
The bounds of cloth
And physiological sanity,
Great buttocks squatted down
On mightier hams than even Herakles,
That puny European free-style he-man
Panting in the shades, his labours lost
To mighty sumo
Who, eyes slit in mounds of face
Grunts and grapples
The Colossus of Nagasaki,
Straining for the fall
Which might just shake
The Earth.

Glory be to he
Whose body mass
Ripples with the moment
Of the muscle wave,
Beating all around the stylish shores
Of calories-composed famine:
See the New man, emaciate, etiolate,
A bean-sprout quiche-thin.

You want him?

More glory be to she
Who encourages cardiovascular stress
In hoping to hoist a sail
On this sea of insurance excess.

When this ship goes down
For the very last time,
What can she do? Cash in.
A doughnut is a life-belt
According
To your point of view.

Mlle. Fifi's Broken Heart

Returning to ze school in England
I saw zees big boys were almost men,
Nineteen, some of zem.
Where previously I ad geeven my all
In ze interests
Of ze French subjunctive,
Now it simmed
Zat only irregular conjugation
Was on zair minds
Wiz advanced-level reference
To more active instruction after school
End no time at all, lately,
For declension.

Presently, ze Ead she say to me,
In ze past, Mam'selle, ze French assistantes
Are eel-favoured, not jolies, end are only titching
grammaire.

She would be most 'appy to 'ear
Of Mam'selle Fifi concentrating
On ze negative
End there was to be no more reference
To zat verb, aimer.

Ah! Cette Anglaise-la!
Doesn't she know
Zat Fifi as only er past participles
To offair
Since Pierre elided wiz Elise
On Fifi's twenty-first
Anniversaire?

Cop Out

He liked them hirsute
The pubes,
Spoke longingly of the Spanish
And their groves,
Yearned to see vast areas
Of no depilation, loth
To acknowledge hysterical despoliation
Of the offensive shorts,
The curlies.
He liked fuzz because he was,
Driving a Thunderbird off-duty
And hoping for vaginal thickets,
An Everglade ever ready
With coverage copious and sprightly
Love-knots,
Black: blondes ain't got
Pubescent forests
Unless
They put on stick-on sheets
Of artificial mats, designed
To meet the approval
Of the policeman on the beat:
Say Heat.

So I showed him my curls, girls
Then went for his blue light:
Delight, until we prised apart.
My pasted on pubes stuck to his
And tore them out, his bikini-line
Waxed bare: I was charged
With defoliating
A moral majority's member.

A defective chief-inspector?
No. Now he likes them nude,
I'm out. Superglued
With Metropolitan shrub
I'm doubly pubed –
Unless the goat's been round and chewed.

A Bit Too Fay

The ladywriter came to see the Ed
And fed him her synopsis:
Her girl is married to the usual selfish fink
Who tied her to the sink at Stonehenge
With some noxious kids who behave badly to those on
                                        DHSS.

He gets in a mess at work and bolts with Dilys, a writer
Who doesn't have to wax her legs, drinks champagne but
                                        worst is slender.
They live on a more ethereal plane but pain is what our
                                        heroine gets.
Stuck with the horrid brats until she meets Dunc
Who though married to Glenda, fills her in on soc-sec form
And more, because sex with Glenda is a bore:
She might be a lesbian, but isn't sure.

Dunc takes his lover on an away-day to the Tor
And before you know it, they're on the sward and working
                                        hard

Prone on Glastonbury's Arthurian vegetation –
This is when she starts vibrating with chthonic
                                        inclination.
Before Dunc can really give her one,
She gets in touch with her core: no more boom-boom for
                                        Dunc;
Her ovaries start holding opinions of their own. Her womb
Spoke. It said 'Don't poke this bloke. Flunk Dunc. You are
                                        the Chosen One
And must abide the Celestial Bunk-up and Cosmic Bun.'

Meanwhile, a wicked politician rides up the road from
                                        Salisbury Plain
Planning the transportation of a bomb by night, right

Across the land. She was skipping round the scenic stones
Primal urges in her bones, breaking through the army's
                                        cordon.
She surged with esoteric power, or was it oestrogenic?
Anyway, the wicked politico saw her and tackled her
Right on a lay line. By now her womb was nice 'nd steady,
Her tubes lubed, ready for the egg of power to flower.
Grunting, grappling with a ping
The Politician entered in and knocked her up.
But gloomy Glenda, Dunc's wife, had at that very moment
Expired, squashed beneath the tyres of a military vehicle:
Very symbolic, if you think about it.
Glenda's soul soared, sought out the object of her
                                husband's defection
And at the moment of conception at the monolith
Tried to kill her with a miasma. She changed her mind
And got the politico instead,
Struck by a dolmen on the head. What a disaster – stone-dead!

So the bomb plot was aborted, but not the sprog,
Ticking away inside her, ready to detonate
At a later date when all her female bits were well plumbed
                                                    in.
Next, she went back to Dunc and secured his aid
In milking the DHSS for vast sums which paid
For cosmetic surgery, turning herself into Dilys
To get her own back on her husband. She ruined them both
To prove something or other, sent the frightful children off
To get finished off at school (salmonella custard for her,
Spontaneous combustion in his rugby boots for him)
And settled down for the Miraculous Birth with Dunc,
Worthy Joseph to her pagan recycled Virgin Queen.

She'd come a long way since North Tidworth,
Had learned of sex and men and when to claim
                                    entitlement
Had listened to the deep mystic bent of her femininity
A hormonal martyr, unhinged,
Waiting for the fission after fusion of her Stonehenge.

She got a glass stable ready for the solar glare
Assembled the animals all female there
Except for Dunc and got ready for the travail
Of the new Saviourette, to give Green significance
To this lay-ette and save us all from the long nuclear
                                                winter.

Oh dear. It all went wrong. The little bastard was a boy
– After all that.
This leads our heroine, whose name was Tracy,
To an insight into a sinister male universe
Where God still ain't a girl
Even if She was once Prime Minister.

Ed said 'It'll never sell,'
But Dunc's deceased-crossed-lesbian wife came back
And poltergeisted Ed from live and unpublishing
To Ed dead
And lady author read.

Brave New World

Name? Age? Degree?
How long a jobbing broker?
Preference: Blonde, Brunette or Me?
Drink? Smoke? Car?
Aerobically Conscious? Credit Card?
Gold? Of course. Stocks, Shares?
Ideal Home and Garden? Au Pairs?
Divorced? Settlement on the Way?
So, Who d'you Lay and Attitude to Sex?
Is that Saturday or Seldom?
Current Pet? If 'Eagle Owl' or 'Guinea Fowl'
Go onto Advanced CV, over there,
For this is an instance
Of Unleaded Care.
Infant Illness? Diseases since?
What Have You Got?
Blood Group, please. Tests Positive
Or Not?

Or Not is OK
Everything else is au fait.
We'll match each other well
According to this questionnaire
Our interior design fits
Like the cap I don't wear.
Bare, it's the Night-Before pill
It's true I haven't tried Spritzers, but I will.
Overall I think you'll agree
That on this data-base I can love you
And when you've been faxed by my CV
You'll note my lack of herpes or squash
So I'm sure that you too, Brian,
Can love me.

Doctor, I Feel So Tired

Bored, I took a toy-boy when the old boy
Failed to come up to scratch.
Kev had an A-level and was resitting
General Science, but what the hell?
A woman can't expect too much
Not looks, youth, and brains as well.
His limbs were trim
His waist was small and going in
Where mine went out and out.
His long fair hair fell over one eye
Half covering an Adonic if pimply pout.
But mostly his thighs were quite a size
Well formed by trys
At Rugby football.

His mother tried to stop it for a start.
Her gratitude was nil, considering
He needed an interest to plug the gap
Once Sixth Form Soccer stopped. I socked it to him,
Showing him
How the organs fitted, A and B
In his Bio text-book, taking the pill and care
To avoid C, the result
Of these two diagrams getting it together
On the page.

To begin with it was risqué, rather frisqué:
His ardour was a thrill until
We topped the National Average (two point five goes a
                                                  week)
Peaking at twice an hour, the point five squeezed in
With fooling in the shower.
Let it be said that he was firing on all his cylinders.

Where Jack was slack, way over the hill
This boy was biking up it, me in tandem
Until I tired and wanted to get off.
It was that
Which spoiled it but first
It was the chat.

He talked about his hamster, how it died
And gloomed. Then there was the spots, the agony
Of acne. We had homework and the tyranny
Of teachers, so weekdays he was in
By ten and then Thursdays, he couldn't miss
Top of the Pops. He collected stamps, kept frogs
And was an Adventure Scout. He called round
And bobbed a job or two in a toggle.
He was callow to the marrow, whining
But not dining me, pocket money being short
And Kevin saving
For a Swiss Army knife, hoping for horses with bunged up
                                                    hoofs
In Acton.
In the meantime he was at it like a rabbit
Like a duck he took to it, me getting wrinkled
Turning grey, praying for time out
For bad behaviour.
While I was getting haggard knackered tense and fraught,
The bastard throve: he thrived on what I'd taught.

Then Jack came back. He had a view
On issues, took me out to dinner, dancing, d-j'd
Me posh-frocked, buying me Bollinger
And roses. In bed he was a gent, intent
On pleasing me, with pauses
For palpitations, and little naps,
Time out to quaff a draught or two
Of Sanatogen, vitamin enriched, acting

Like jump-leads. Stately, it was lovely.
Slow. I knew a glow
Of relief: but grief
Was to be my portion.

Where my interests lay these Jackless days
He gently tried to find, 'You were a lady, I recall,' he said
'Who had a lively mind.'

I opened up my mouth for adult intercourse:
Out flew hamsters, homework, spots,
The joy of stamps, Kylie, Madonna, keeping frogs
Having fun hiking, going on about biking
The Top Ten and then the unfairness
Of the UCCA system. I talked transformers, Gazza, Coe,
Model airplane kits, Neighbours and so to the evanescent
                                                          wit
Of the Beverly Hills Cops – out it all popped, dreary all,
                                                          dire:
Boring. Jack gently shut the door.
I heard his Porsche leaving, roaring, leaving me

To young Spotty.

He was drawing up on his new moped
Wearing an anorak, a fully-fledged
Sex maniac with the strength of ten
And time to fit in sixfold before East End
-Ers.

And what's that doctor?
School hols soon? Yes, You're right,
And Kev's Mum's permission
For him to stay at night.

Brief Encounter

He took off his coat, hat, scarf, gloves, jacket and shoes.
I removed mine.
He took off his socks.
I removed my tights.
He undid his belt.
I undid mine.
He loosened his stock-broker red braces.
I took off my pearls.
He removed his tie.
I took off my earrings.
He undid his shirt.
I dropped my skirt.
He unzipped his trousers.
I unbuttoned my blouse.
He took off his watch.
So did I.
He pulled his vest over his head.
I loosened my chemise.
He took off his boxers.
I took off my bra.
That left me with my knickers on.
He took them off;
But we couldn't remember why,
So we got dressed again.

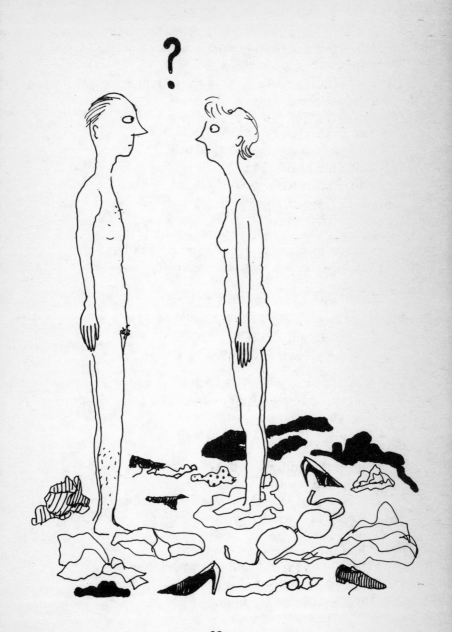

Not Now

Not when I'm brushing the stairs
And all I can see is the mess,
And bending down making the bed, dear,
Is not the best time for congress.

I don't like it down in the kitchen
With you and the veg on the boil.
Last time I kicked a pan off the oven
Full of chips and smoking hot oil.

No, I know that you never noticed
Because you too were seething with lust,
But it was me with my foot in the cat's bowl
While your view was obscured by my bust.

I think we can rule out the garden
Since next door's cut a peephole to spy,
It's always me with my back to the earthworms
When I catch the mad roll of his eye.

It's dangerous when I've been knitting
You know you got caught up in four ply,
And you were lucky, sitting nude on my needles,
To only get stabbed in the thigh.

The bathroom's quite out of favour
For bondage with *that* sort of rope,
It's too short, and the language is uncalled for
Just because you fell when you slipped on it's soap.

I find the front room's too formal.
The pile on the rug makes my back sore
Besides, I can lip-read the telly, vol: off
Upside down on the floor.

Not now my darling, not ever.
I'm sick of your lust-crazed face
And I'd like to escape from your clutches,
From your rough, tough and hairy embrace.

You see dear I've been made an offer
Concerning celibacy and money, a lot:
He's eighty and rich with no sex drive
But thankgod he's still got his yacht.

The First Deadly Sin

Miss Frimm went to church a lot
But after her mother and her budgie died
Felt God had forgotten her, been unkind.
While Ma and Bluie lived, she didn't mind
So much
Spinster-hood: at any rate, she'd kept the shelf
Well polished. Though she was plain, wore glasses
And hid herself in crimplene, it didn't mean
Her heart was dead.
No, only dormant.

Too late. Mother was eighty-eight and ailing
For many years. Miss Frimm in duty never failing
Rushed home each day from Action Station
Where she'd worn a uniform in the ticket office
And wished she too could pick her destination
Like the travellers hurrying through
To Epping, Ongar, Waterloo
While she came home direct to Mother
And her little blue pet budgerigar.
Bus 207 brought her back each day
To No. 11, Balfour Way, W13, to meet her Fate.
Fit, fat, retiring early for Mummy's sake
Her life slipped slowly by. No man came
To claim her.

Alone in her small parlour now
She looks out through the crisp net curtains
At how the families opposite have grown,
The children leaving, having children of their own
Yet for Miss Frimm life stands forever still.
The clock ticks on the mantelpiece
The leaves fall down from the London limes outside

To mark the passage, the rustle of Time
And sighing, her polyester bosom rising
She's filled with wild, impossible yearnings
Inappropriate.

Then by came Stan, the window-cleaner.
Stalwart, sixty, a cheeky chappy, leaner
Than a garden rake. He caught Miss Frimm
One day in disarray, ringing her bell
When she was in the bath. She came down flushed
To the door. Her glasses steamed.
And so did Stan. From the path he caught a glance
Of what he lacked in life: female comeliness.
Miss Frimm's flesh was pink and fresh, preserved,
Unused, her body curved out in luscious billows
Of tender roundness, moist from the water, her breast
Two pillows of Tog.10 apiece.
How he longed to rest his tired head!
Tongue-tied for once, he cleared his throat
And asked for the window-cleaning money instead.

Next time, prepared, he was more adroit.
Asking for water in his bucket, he came right in
From there to inside cleaning. He polished up
The stained glass in the hall, with the door open
So all the neighbours saw Stan, soaping away
In a manner beyond reproach.
Besides, they knew Miss Frimm. A figure of gentle fun,
                                        prim,
They pitied her, knew her mum and budgie gone
And thought it fine
That Stan should take the time
To talk to her: they were always meaning to pop in
For a chat, but busy lives and this and that
Led only to neighbourhood watching
From a distance, through the nets.

33

Meanwhile Stan polished, cleaned and twinkled round the
place
Playing a part in the squeegying of her heart,
That dusty receptacle hidden by a British Home Stores
cardigan
And they got on well.
Discreetly, gently, their love began to swell
And grow: a day trip to Windsor, a visit to the zoo
As far as Bognor by the sea, Surrey, eventually
They went all round Middlesex
And back for tea.

No-one knew how once a month they stoked the fires
On the crochet bed-spread, desires held in by velvet curtains
On a pole, choking on an eiderdown soft
With plumped-up runnels, just like Miss Frimm.

After glow, Stan would tidy up, polish bed-knobs,
Brass and fender to show his love. He burnished up the tiles
The ornaments, the wooden tables, wardrobes shone
With polish. All gleamed, all cleaned by Stan
In spirit reverential
That so much pulchritude at last
Should come his way, a humble window-cleaning man.

Miss Frimm, content, visited her mother's grave.
She put down a bloom or two as the cars roared through
Looking for the M4 slip road, last exit from Brentford,
Offering a prayer to the lead polluted air, she explained.
'I'm sorry Mother, I know it's not exactly ecumenical
My carry-on with Stan, but we get on a treat.
And after all,' she sighed with satisfaction,
'I've got the cleanest windows in the street.'

For this sin of Pride, the Deity squashed her
Under a passing No. 65.

(Stanley went back to his wives. He was a bigamist anyway.)

Doggerel

Motherhood:
It done her good.
It made her bosom saggy
And her face all haggy.

Her hair fell off her head
But grew instead
Upon her chin.
Her bones were thin
And she had stretch marks on her skin.

Her ankles exploded,
Her innards imploded,
She had varicose veins,
Heartburn pains.
And bunged up drains.

AM's she threw up
Wearing support cups,
PM's she couldn't sleep
Restless under the heap,
Endocrinely unstable, she'd weep.

She got cystitis,
Moles and vaginitis,
Her nipples cracked
And she was racked
By lack of alcohol when she was whacked.

He sailed through sublime
And at her time
Told her when to scream
Puff and pant: it seemed
That fatherhood had been his dream

After birth he couldn't wait
To re-impregnate.
But his plans of tribalness were pipped
When she had him and his trousers permanently zipped.
In his sleep, she had him snipped.

She was a vet
Who knew what she meant
By pet.

Zoo

He took up all the room in the double bed,
He snored, whimpered in his sleep
And if she complained, nearly bit her head off.
He never smelled nice, unless done up
For something special, like a show:
My word! Then he was well-groomed and manicured,
Off he'd go, for the benefit of fluffy bits of stuff
Without a brain between them
He was affectionate in his way
And would hold her down and slobber on her face.
She was afraid to move or speak
Because his temper like his tail was short.
He could shut her up by merely rolling over:
Twelve stone ten he was to her eight
And soon she began to hate him
Though her friends went on about his liquid lovely eyes
Said he was well built, intelligent too:
He knew a thing or three but not, it seemed,
The use of dental floss.
To be frank, his breath was rank.
She felt it was no loss
When she shipped him off to Canada
To herd the moose. 'You bitch',
His look inferred as they carted him off
But something in her stirred. She rejoiced.
Free, she settled down alone in bed,
Her rotten rottweiler gone –
Then she missed him.

She got herself a man instead.

He took up all the room in the double bed,
He snored, whimpered in his sleep

And if she complained, nearly bit her head off.
He never smelled nice, unless done up
For something special, like a show:
My word! Then he was well-groomed and manicured,
Off he'd go, for the benefit of fluffy bits of stuff
Without a brain between them – etc.
Ergo, this rotten rotter she got rid of too
And settle down to live alone
With an oyster:
Rugged, handsome, not violent,
This silent shellfish was not selfish.
When he had a hangover he was never peeved
If she relieved him
Of his pearl.
This suave mollusc knew
How to treat a girl.

Gaga Saga

She got married to a right-on sort of man,
Someone in computers and a stripey shirt, a capitalist
On the make and after a honeymoon in Bermuda,
They bought a serious fifteen bedroom mansion
With a barbecue and a tennis court.
Once they'd bull-dozed the knot garden,
They planned to fill it with jacuzzis,
Doberman dogs, a little analyst or super tycoonette:
She read the book, hired the Harley Street man
Then urged her Brian on.

Success, of course. Banged up, she gave up work
And repaired with an au pair to await the birth.
She was calm and maddeningly hale,
No throwing up for her, no balloon legs,
Or intolerable tightness of being.
She power-dressed right up to sixth months
Then eased, complaining, into a size twelve.
And then the birth. She did it under water, you know.
The poor little blighters had to swim for it
To the strains of Mozart and some grunting.
In fact she grunted even more when she saw them:
There were three. Old Harley Street, stoned, had missed
them
On his screen.

Well, she threw a fit. One she had figured, but three!
You couldn't even get three on, it was all shift work.
The au pair left, overwhelmed. The nannies wouldn't
stay
Because of her. Brian took care to be out all day
Only returning when they were washed and stacked
away at night.

Weekends he worked a lot
Mostly on Linda, common as muck but tax deductible
Whom he set up in a bunker at the Barbican,
Not far from Scargill's gaff.

The house was filled with nappies, rusks and buggies,
Rompers, bottles, teething-rings, pins. There was
                                        gripewater,
Pappy food to lick, packs of esoteric mixes, sterilising
                                                    gear
And lots of sick. There was screams, shouts and treble
                                                wailing.
She was failing to do her face or nails, wore jeans
And didn't change for dinner, being involved
In dribbly mucky operations where she laced the three
With quarts and gallons squished out of either end.
Brian eventually could not stand the sight
And took promotion and flight to Florida
Six months in the year.

Out one day pushing two and carrying one, like a squaw,
She went down the village and across a field
Saw her salvation: Farmer Roddy. He saw her,
Fecund, natural, she looked a treat
Standing haggard near the sheep.
Just what he wanted to warm his bed.
She saw a mighty giant, rugged, poor, bristling
With ginger nosehairs and virile intent.

To him, the babies were a treat: he picked 'em up
In hands of spam and treated them like little lambs
Two on the bottle, one getting burped, he never shirked
The dirty work. He took them with him out to harrow
And left them coralled by his collie Sue.
Three on a knee, he loved to dandle them
Laughing, hirsute, he made a lovely daddy,

But not theirs. Back came Brian and made a scene
Got custody and bore them off.
He married Linda, to be their nurse
Then had a vasectomy without first telling her.
He wanted glamorous not mammarous glands
And let her think she was unable.

But she was not. She met Roddy in the stable:
Score three more with ginger hair.
Brian knew this wasn't playing fair
And went back to keep wife number one
Who has started up her own knitwear factory
Based on local exploitation, cheap labour and Roddy's
                                        sheep.

Linda and Roddy kept their three
But the first batch were snatched away to school
Paid for by their yuppy mum and dad who couldn't find
The heart or time to finish what they'd freely started.
Bri and his wife lived à la mode. He made more money.
She wrote a book on celibacy, its merits, and went on TV
Wogan. A star, but not another child was born.

Were they punished? Dear Reader, just wait and see –
The word to conjure with is: Puberty.
You see, you think you beget children
But they get you
– Eventually.

Shorts Shrift

Their fathers fought them on the beaches
And now it's hot town, mortars in the city;
War-weary in camouflage parrot fatigues
The lady Brits launch, blending tropically or not
With the gothic staunch façade
Of Oxford Street.
The amazon saxon strides out
Shorted, hinting as she comes
Of the fear of battleships, bazooka-breasted,
A grey frigate or two, armed:
Multinationally she waddles, the Rose,
A Side-winder or Exocet in her handbag,
Ready for the tourists' guns.

Blast them off the beats, babes,
Heave them hearty with your well-armed
Rear admirables lurching along.
They've never seen such hearts of oak
Bottoming out, for fundamentally
Avoirdupois is all, the tonnage of a tank
The momentum of a carrier, Ark,
Royal thighs the size of which
Wipe out the eyes of foreign guys
All thin, all benefiting from Benettonic
Tone, their feet Guccied, their cameras Fuji-flexed.

Stuff your Deutsche mark, stick your yen
And take off boys: you've only seen the women:

Are you gung-ho enough to face
The men?

Slack Beauty

Born the apple of her parents' eye
You never saw a child so young
Blessed by the Star of Beauty high
From the cradle to that place, slender,
Cheeks flushed by sweet winds
Face douce, hair fair, lips
Petal-soft and tender.

Being woman, she was fine and she was tall
Long-throated, willowy, straight like a queen
She moved among them all;
But she moved alone did Beauty
Walking like the Night,
Too perfect to have women friends,
Too beautiful to be right.

And the men feared her,
The universal dream-girl
About whom they fantasised
Pacing in her blemishless pale flesh
Before their callow eyes.
They dreaded her for a goddess
And settled for pretty, which they understood
But not pretty enough to be odd.
They thought to pair with her somewhere
Would probably be a god.

So all she ever got was connoisseurs
The men of easy money, gold,
Who realised her for an asset,
Bought her, stroked her, petted for a time
Then sold.

The lovely lady cried
And she wept within her head:
'Oh let me be old and equal, Lord,
Or please let me be dead'.

No-one cared for the lonely woman
Inside her pearly shell.
But should a tart get diamonds, furs, my husband
And still find love as well?

Nice for Norah

The girls get together.
Survivors of birthings,
Victims of earth-movings
And orgasmic icing –
So what do they say? Varicose veins, the pains
Of the latest Fergie Fondu or HRT?
Their husbands' corporeal struggle?
The way their daughters
Do what they never oughter?
More recipes and slagging off
Her Next Door? More?
Politics and his mother?
Blather
Blether. Bore?
Never.

It's the career; Maria,
The flat in Spain: Jane,
The eye-job on the bags,
Six weeks in shades for Suit Case Lil;
The screw in the new reg. car,
The policeman flashing only his torch
And pinking at what he's thinking
Is the Women's Institute heavy
Getting groped: but it's not,
It's the gardening boy, Derek,
Delving for Doreen
With his dibber.

Maggy likes Mahler, Hannah Henry or is it hemp?
Mary's head's turned red: henna.
But Thelma went to Afghanistan once.
She wore a veil and failed to advise
The Russians. The Mujaheddin and their goats
Were nice.

Hortensia wants to put on more weight.
At only thirteen stone she's thin to the bone,
An endangered species, the roll-mop Raphaelite.
Gloria's a finished Go-go girl
Whose husband went: he found the tassels
She claimed were earrings. Domestic hassles
And tales of pasties flying off into the sheriff's eye
In Pasadena, not Peckham Rye.

Wimmin torque? Babies and maybes
Is done by men. No Dworkins dworked here,
No Weldon welded. They steer clear
Of the Greer-role –
Fifty's not a speed-limit.
It's a goal.
Ask Joan.

Abelard

I flushed I blushed I had thrush.
I'd work up a sweat
And lie down fluttering faint
In the throes of sexual restraint.
My simple harmonic motion
Lay dead on the bed
De-sexed.
Oh yes.

This is it: the end.
I'd warmed to my role young
When pubic hair announced
Biology. I've shown it to many.
Any endorphin upsurge
Then gave me the urge
Of an athlete
Whose Fosbery
Never flopped.

It's stopped. The wingèd chariot's
Impinged creaking on the timer.
It's pinged.
To procreate was great
But it's finished, over.
I'll now spend my sands more gladly
In grunting over the Guardian
Or walking the tosa.

I'm nearly almost practically forty-two.
I abdicate the sexual treadmill to you.
Plod it on your own,
Or learn to knit.
Testosterone degeneracy
Is OK by me.

47

A View to a Pill

Happy the health hunter, happy she
Who goes down Holland and Barrets
For Vitamin C.
If your hair is lank or your face all spotty
Take brewers yeast: B6 and 12 if premenstrually potty
Plus four capsules of Evening Primrose Oil
While in it's grip to take your temper
Off the boil.
If your intestines are giving you jip,
Five garlic pearles. Extract of peppermint
Two mls at night
Will say farewell to colonic blight.
You squint?
'A' every day, but not too much!
It turns you yeller
And that, plus the garlic,
May alarm your feller, so B-complex for lots of sex.
Feel renally restrained?
Then bladder wrack and get it out.
Take lots of zinc and calcium for gout:
If you don't your hair and then your brains fall out.
Rub 'E'
Into the stretch marks on your tum.
Take four hundred I.U.'s of Vitamin D
To supplement the lack of winter sun.
And pound outsize thighs with cod liver oil.
This will increase your bum's lipidity
(But do it in private, unseen by kitty).
Copper and Iron, Selenium,
Magnesium is lots of fun:
Take it in handfuls, as it comes.
Lastly you'll need Folic Acid,
At least one hundred mgs.

For the anaemia you contract in pregnancy:
With all this pill-taking,
You forgot just one.

Oh'd

'Oh frock!
I clocked you in the sale
Hanging a hundred pounds half-price
Upon the rail.
Frothy you were, with lace
To frame the winter-weary face,
Small pearl buttons,
Godet pleats, a neat plastron
And a little bow, velvet,
Upon the sit upon.
A size too small, but what the hell?
I only started up to swell
At Christmas.'

And thus, poor mortals, with a receipt
Do we nourish our self-deceit,
Murmuring, 'Self-discipline will soon begin.
The diet starts on Monday.'
And so you pray that it will fit one day.
Woman, know thyself:
All thy piety and wit cannot disguise
This pure bull-shit.

French for Starters

It was Mary's première: She had to get it right,
Set la table expansively avec choice choses
Des Roses, chandelles, light fronds,
Granny's best argent, Mum's Crown Derby,
Aunty's hand-embroidered Italian linge,
Next doors goblets de crystal, Gary upstairs
His Giacometti-style chaises, difficult to sit on
But looking chic. The nourriture was copié
From top-notch magazines, you'd never seen
Such bon yum-yums, if you liked minceur:
A sprig of oregano, un pot de crème
And a Kiwi fruit, quails –
Poor little things, their petites pattes
Dangled in the pomme de terre purée, like corpses on a
                                                shroud
But she was proud of them. She'd plucké et stuffé them
                                                herself
With a magnifying mirror and a pair of tweezers.
She had something flambé planned for pud,
It all looked good: Trevor ought to get a rise for this
When the boss came pour diner.

But sa femme came aussi; she'd once done this too,
Got rid of her Trev and snapped up the patron
On the strength of her fondue.
Out of jalousie she always undermined
The morale of those with whom they dined.
The ladies se regardaient, then they began.
Mrs Boss a laissé tomber a glass of sherry
And ruined Aunty's cloth with charm. The canapé, she
                                        was heard to say
Was dross and harmful to her palate: she quailed at quail
And asked for some fromage instead.

Our hostess, nothing loth, spilled gravy down her dos
Found mousetrap and pared off the vert before serving it
On a salver, whipping off the lid with un flourish
                                        sarcastique.
Madame B. a demandé if the lumps in the purée
Was the nourissement rising visiblement to the top
And Trevor had to stop the response, involving une carotte
                                        hot.
Come the dessert, Madame passed on the chocolate soufflé
And fanned it with her eyelashes faux so it sank
But Mary's Bombe Surprise nearly blew her wig off,
Mary substituting chile for ginger in the sauce, au dernier
                                        moment.
Comment they all laughed at that one, surtout le Boss.
When the crèpes appeared, the guest jogged Mary's elbow
And the flambé spread and nearly brought the house down
But they put it out with precocious french eaux
They'd got in especially to make a show.
Everything was ruined, as Madame had sought, all brulé
So she went chez eux early, singed but victrix
As she thought.

Monsieur le Patron stayed behind,
Followed Trev and Mary into the nouvelle cuisine
To share les saucissons explosives and mash they'd been
Itching to chomp, instead of putting on the posh.
The patron sighed: said he'd not seen such nosh for
                                        longtemps
Since his exec-wife forced him to faire regime.
They tucked right in, with beaucoup de HP sauce of course
And had tinned peaches in evap. lait for pud.
In verité, it did Boss good
But not poor Trev: he was saqué anyway.
Boss thought him crude. Right from the beginning
He'd seen him breathing on his Vichyssoise to try to warm it.

He'd got no goût. The rest had all been fun, but time to go!
He payed Trev off et a fait l'amour à Mary, who had a
                                                    plan.

The ex-exec and the ex exec-wife were both divorcés
And Mary a épousé the Boss, un gros cochon.
She fed him up until il a explodé, cholesterol in his veins
Then re-married Trev and took on the ex-wife as bonne.
You see, rich young Mary needed quelqu'un
Pour échanger des violents recipes avec
So now they all have lots of joie
Se slinging jars of caviare and foie gras:
They're what's referred to as ménage à pois.

The Anorexic Tee-totaller

I didn't want to eat the poor little animals any more
And went veggy: I got the cook-book
And took a look at the fibrous way of life,
Putting away my knife, cleaver and steak bashers,
The things for skewering snails and ripping off ducks' flippers
And my Arabian sheep's eye-ball grippers.
I thought I'd need a slicer and a skillet,
A wooden porringer and lots of green stuff to fill it.
My eggs were free range: I knew the hens
Would be un-penned, then pensioned but not puréed off.
The milk and cheese and mooey stuff
Came from contented cows.
So now I was ready for a life without internal strife,
No dilemma, no ethical or moral blame.
Shame about the book, then.
I turned the pages.
'With a very sharp knife,' it said, 'poke out
The eyes of the black-eyed beans.
Seize the tomatoes and bereave them of their seeds.
Freeze. Grind the peppercorns small small small
Then haul the chives from their little pot
And cut 'em up. Slice and dice, that's nice
Make the little green juices flow: go and get
Some eggs. Break them into a bowl
And beat them – hard.
Slash the mushrooms
So they fall down flat, stalkless in Stanmore,
Then stuff them.
Boil oil and fry: listen to them squeaking
As they die so you'll know they're done.
Skin, thrash or mash a spud,
Eviscerate and broil a capsicum
For now your omelette you have begun.'

  – This was just the first course: I had yet to get
The fruit.

Faint, appalled at the thin edge of the wedge
That violent cooks dish out to veg,
I reached for a beaker full of the warm South,
Full of the true, the blushful Hippocrene
With beaded bubbles winking at the brim –
It was on the sink, just by the Vim.

But should I swig it and perpetuate
The Great Fruitarian and Vegetable Rape,
Knowing what they do to grapes?
Of course not: Oh yes, and I'm celibate too.

     I just haven't got the strength for you.

A Barre Too Far

'You can do it, oh yes you can!
Get your foot up, on the top barre
Then see how far
You can bring your chin to your shin –
Feel the pain? Just take the strain.
Backs straight,
Supporter leg
Firm!'

The instructress bends her rubber limbs
And turns herself inside out.
A cart-horse to her colt
I stand fluorescent, in my kit,
Lycra'd to the hilt,
A glowing neon presence
In footless tights,
A monument to chips, late nights
And female metabolic mayhem.

Get your leg up?
I'll be lucky to get it over, at this rate,
But Caroline says it's OK
So long as I open out the groin
And never mind the poin.
It'll help in childbirth, later.
I'll shell them out like peas
Leg up, firing 'em at the doc –
But now, bend, so
Down you go, fatso: sweat, twist and take it on the chin,
For thankfully, eight o'clock soon comes
And it's home
For intravenous gin.

Not Much Going On

A flat in Docklands:
An old warehouse done out in white
With all the bricks on show
And huge windows showing the Thames
And, well, being England, rain.
We live minimally, dressed in black,
Him with his hair pulled back, an ear-ring
Me blonde as I can go
Without my hair snapping off,
Ears weighted like a Masai warrior's
With esoteric art: varnished foetuses might be in
But I'm worried they'll clash
With my gear nouveau, Gautier and co,
My big boots comme il faut and right tight tube skirt.
Call myself Ms Purple now.
Not Angela Brown, that's naff.
No, I'm Purple Patch,
Working for designer TV
Where you can see me see me see me
Looking chilled and talking clever
In three minute bursts
To the Boys in the Band don't ask me
Don't ask me who: they all wear leather,
Blue jeans. Like we're all James Dean
Down at the studio.
But here, Thor and I
(Claims he's Scandinavian
But it's more like Scouse)
Have set up High Tech House
Away from Retro: except for the jazz,
That is, and I'll go as far as Schoenberg
If pushed.

If pushed, we fall into a futon
And eat sushi take-away, drinking Schlob or Schlatz,
Looking through the *Face*
To see to see to see if we
Are more minimal this week than last.
Thor's got an exhibition soon:
Spatial he is, with his use
Of inner tubes:
Like we've all got inner tubes, right?
And some gonna get punctured, right?
Or at least deflate gently: yeah,
It's a metaphor on our floor at the moment
For like,
You know, Life –

Couldn't imagine, when I was doing GCSE,
That I'd be living a designer life myself
You know, like, really minimally.

Neighbourhood Watch

What do they do in there so quiet?
Why don't they racket like the last lot, riot,
Play rock music
And hold loud parties?

Why don't they scream and shout like we do,
Hopelessly in love and out abusing each other
In the garden? From the loo?
They don't even call their cats by name.
No-one came in a year to visit,
No phone, no moan of anything
From ardour to anguish:
They languish.

I see her coming home,
Then he goes in.

Then there's the silence,
The absence of din.

Shh! Can you hear it?
There it is, nothing –

He must be doing it to her again.

Family Planning

Connubials with care:
No left foot in the air
For reclines Jones, a ginger cat
And we are bare.
Sit up for a sip of tea
And see Lily purr onto the pillowslip
With Jessy, her brat.
Try and recline diagonally
On top of me, melded
With the toast-crumbs
Of a good weekend lie-in:
So far, a layoff.
Try again. More bumping bums,
Feeling for fusion. Confusion.
Jones bites the duvet
Causing mortis in your vigour,
Lily leans out and flays
My nose while Jessy is down the sheet
Grappling a stray nipple:
We go for mutual bleat.
The wolfhound bounds barking on the bed;
Further collapse of flaccid party,
– No gropes for these dopes.
Then it's the rabbit, Anthrax,
Insisting on Cornflakes
And chewing the electric blanket.
In comes Kong the gerbil,
He wants bacon and egg
Then the stick insect
Who likes mice
And the mice who likes Twiglets: Problem.
Conjugals are cancelled
When the RSPCA calls

To find a foster home
For a ferret.

Your brow darkens with exasperation.
'This Ark on our Saturday bed
Causes testicular constipation:
Let's go to the bathroom instead,
Steam, bubbles and no menagerie
Often leading, ultimately, to breeding'

Karma.

He gets in the tub.
By the time I turn round.
For a scrub

He's gone:
Forgot
To spot
The piranha.

A Pencil Must Be Lead

I gaze forlornly at the object
Of no inspiration.
It studies the floor.
The cat eyes it askance,
Clears off. Better chance
On the compost heap,
Something mantis not mentis.

Show it the knickers with the aero-flow
Then go for the thermo-nuclear
Body-suit. It's worked before.
Shut the door and return
To study of the grey area.

It's brooding transcendentally
With a Ph.d. in the sin
Of omission, Groucho
Sans glasses, real low.

I shout at it,
It shirks.
I coo,
It lurks.
I read to it,
It snores,
I sing to it,
It's bored
And reclines
Like a swine
Who declines
To truffle.

I tickle, I torque,
I scratch, I balk,
I scream, I swear
And still it's just bare
-ly there.

Give up. Get the papers,
Make the tea
And whaddya know?
The racing results
Do help it to grow.

It rears up at fences
Throwing handicap off:
Carsen, Cauthen, Pat Eddery and Co,
Walter Swinburne, Lanfranco Dettori –
Do these men know
They make it grow faster
Than my best crutchless
Knicker-knocker show?

It comes on a length, smirking,
A perked up little gherkin
Who throws off dejection
And goes for selection,
Nap.

It thinks I'm a filly. Silly.
Snorting at hurdles
Curdles this mare.
Vaginismus nobbles it: hurt pride
Hobbles it.

The thing gets the chop:
                    Whop:
                    Off with its head.

Despite racing features
It's met its own Bechers;
It's got a dud stud's excuse
Next time,
Not to trot,
So – Piggot.

In Extremis

Here come the heavy-handed cats:
They also pace who only stand
And weight, for muscle in motion to begin.
They've studied hard, these guys,
These brisk firm dolls, advanced,
Strutting their stuff
And warming to the class.
All mean men here, the women lean
Athletes, runners, marathon crunchers:
The unfit flab-bags hunch down over weights
Or reel exhausted from the stretch
To watch in awe
For here he comes, the Prince of Pecs;
He picks his way, Ashanti war-lord
Thro' the ranks of the body warriors
Who lurch and sweat at his command, wet;
Sinews scream, the biceps bulge,
We teeter on the edge of cardiac arrest
And that's only me in a Lycra vest
Watching ringside.
Wow! Winston! Killer-man!
You're a six-six gleaming beauty, black:
I'm a five foot female slug and slack,
Your lats and glutes all cause dismay
For if I join the class,
Will I too not stick out all over
One happy Arnold Schwarzenegger
Doppelganger Day?

More Tea, Vicar?

My darling was ethnic minority.
He wanted dhal.
I cooked kippers and custard,
Chips marmaladé and Yorkshire crud.
He awaited the flurry of curry;
I gave him boiled-for-a-week greens
And a spud.
He lusted after mango kulfi, cold
So he got rhubarb brisket, tuna,
And gravy geometrical, old.

He accused me of colonicism,
Said he needed a tandoori houri,
Not one pail-based.
He longed for chole with chilly
But the new girl gave him suet pastry
To the point of a prostate rebore.
She came from Punjab
And knew
What hard lard was for.

Did I tell you he was Irish?
Well, he turned cardinal
And had us
En-nunned.

Bunning jellied-leather squid bhaji,
Me and Ranjit covenanted together
Like a culinary house on fire:
His will be one day
Because
Our highest and holiest gourmet desire
Is to see the white friar fried,
The Carmelite
Flambé.

Centric

The importance of Moi
And my genes
Means
That the Human Race
May yet be won.
Therefore
The crime second to none
Is murder,
In case
The ex-gene bearer
Is not just any old sod
But neo-god.

Not of York

I fink Shakespeare, that long-winded john
Wiv 'is Macbefs 'n' 'at's absurd –
All Stratford grammar school 'e was
Wiv 'is loads a 'words words words.'

Linguistically I goes furver back than 'im.
I goes Saxon 'cos all we needed then an' still
Is yer ethnic shorts like 'slaughter', 'stab' an' 'kill'.
It's back to British basics we gotta go
'Cos eff 'n' blind is wot us moderns know.
It was only yer normals, yer bloody Frogs
Wot give us posh, an' where they get aristo tosh?
Off yer Romans, that bleedin' Eyetie latin lot.

Don' patronise the workin' man wiv no long words
Play it on 'is stereo: give it 'im mono, give it 'im low
Sell 'im sleaze-bag sex an' sell 'im lager,
Make his mental engrossment 'arder.
It's wot 'e wants an' it befits 'im for 'is station,
Like wot it done for me: Oxbridge,
A marxist professor of education.

All Shakespeare give 'is lot was 'amlet,
That Danish bum.
I want to give our lot
The sun.

Always Somewhere

I am Rosie and my legs ache
From working in the bar
Because I have to,
Taking up with other women's men, sometimes,
Because that's the way I am.
I like to give. They take.
In my warm arms they find, sometimes,
A way out from detergent-clean wives.
I'm not nice, like they are.
My hair's a mess, with the bleach
And my eyes are tired, under the black
And I have no coy children, wishing
I am a TV mum. Empty.
I am a liar but I lie mostly
To myself.

I am a woman
Of a certain age.
My past is dark
But my future's known. Tonight home
With your boy
Who likes a bit of slack
Then he's back
To you.

Have 'im pet: no regret.
For me, tomorrow and tomorrow
And tomorrow creeps in this petty pace
To the last syllable of recorded 'Time gentlemen, please'
To bring me yet another
Lady's man.

Ask him and see
If he don't deny me.
Then you'll know for sure
That what I'm telling you
Is true.

Ph. D-Day

The Past has passed
Irretrievably,
The Future fails to exist
Existentially.
Even Now
Is Not
By the Time
You've got
      Round to it.

        Speaking metaphorically, my love
        You ain't
        Therefore our union
        Is quaint.
        Ergo,
        Go.
            Piss off.

Bimbo in Limbo

She sun-bedded for him, fat-free,
Giving up gin for beautiful skin
Hair flossed with perox, arm-pits leached bare
So that in going for the conjugular
Not one excresence follicular existed
To cause him despair.
Teeth bleached to a dazzle, chins lipo-suctioned off,
The new hoover-remover pared her down
To perfection.

Along comes Tess, chops chewing on chips
Face sallow, bristle-shinned, she's moustached.
With under-arm thickets, she last saw past her bust
At sixteen, a stereo pair, D-cup obliterating navel
But leading uniformly
To lust.

He went for her, driven by chthonic urges
In his new BMW: carnalistic on cue,
Tess was ably atavistic yet hirsutely heuristic.
Screaming like a dream when in full fat-so throe,
Her inorganic role was simply cathartic,
And not in any way
Arctic.

So wallow, willow, on your pillow
Or sweat, grunt, get thawed –
For he who starts with a coupé
Always ends up
With a Ford.

After Saddam

Alice, fourteen, winter sunlight on fair hair,
Kneeling beneath the Christmas tree,
Looking up at him, smiling up at him
Thro' curtains of sheer and shining courtesan locks,
Her eyes brown slits
with sudden knowledge
And on her lips
The Giaconda smile
Of any woman who ever knew
Mastery over men.
Alice, fourteen, proffering her first fruits, coquette,
At the tips of her schoolgirl fingers,
Not yet complete in her strengths
But gauging this man's needs
As she rises up
From ribbons and wrapping paper,
Knowing that one day soon
He will take up this apple invisible
And bite into it.
This man, soldier, watching
This child insinuate herself between his knees
For the Christmas kiss;
Her hands light, the fingers linger
Upon the one leg flesh, the other Gulf War steel.
This child, slender, godiva hair falling down, bending down
To kiss
Her uncle
Her uncle
Afraid
Of Alice, fourteen.

Morning Glory

I rarely say this:
No man cares to wear
His heart on his sleeve
But I want you to know
The love that I grow
Is for you.

Take the choice blooms
Which I lay at your feet.
Let me kiss press hug you to me
So my propinquity speaks,
Mere units of spoken language
Fail to express
The depth of devotion
I feel on caress.

Sweetheart, sweet word,
I love you almost enough
To make you my wife:
Please get up, get dressed
And go out. Get *The Sporting Life*.

Daffodil

The quiet boy smiled past me
And it touched his eyes.
I saw him across the bar, in the glass,
Saw the light glint down on him.
Glimmer on his hair, fair,
Across the bar, in the glass.

Through the looking-glass
I fell in love every night
People drinking, laughing in the happy hour
Washing off the sadness of their lives
Or loves, like me, bar-flies
Tacky in the webs, laughing in the happy hour.

Talking quietly to his pals, the noisy boys,
He falls silent. Leaning on the juke-box
He's looking through the smoke
Through the looking-glass
But catching my eye his skeeters away
Like it always does, looking through the smoke.

But he raises his glass across the bar
And the shy boy smiles again
Past my misted face, like on every night:
Unfocussed, his gaze goes through me to the mirror
For the shy smile that touches his eyes
Touches only his own heart, like on every night.

Paranoia

Pass through the portals, Temple of the Arts,
Seeking the deliberate understatement
In artistic intervention: it's on the floor,
Some orange irons or bits of pipe
With potential for variation, despite
It's indefinity of type. It seems
That the configuration of ground-based beams
Invests it with a broody, slabby sense
Of order.

Thinking 'fenders' on first appraisal,
You pursued your Philistian right until you saw
That these insistent concepts were specially spatial
Not brute, not paltry, not poorly painted
Floating blobs.

Post past our modern eloquence, hang a right and go,
Be brave: front
The J. Constable country bumpkin show.

I mean, what's he got?
Trees, sky and water, a lot.
He daubs a boy fishing, two damn donkeys
And a dog.

A Suffolk swede, well past his sell-by date, RA
For such slops in oil and a thing for leaves today
The boy'd do therapy, if not Time,
Saving us his unintensive farming,
His rambling lanes, cloud-clime, lock-block.
He for whom I emote is poor grand-dad:
Clots like Constable was all the art he had.

In this foyer I've got girder grandeur,
And quite frankly
I am glad.

Axiomatic

Was it worth it, Mary, for your Earl, girl,
To sit ever after the guest
Of that elusive landlady, Elizabeth,
The cold seeping up your royal Stuart bones
And your flesh wizening,
Knowing no man's hand? Was it worth it?
Did love's ghost sustain you, lady,
Plotting still down the grey English years
Of most solitary confinement,
Your crown of thistles plucked from you
By those who protested your lack
Of catholic taste in men? Was it worth it?
And when they brought the news:
Bothwell dying mad in Denmark, that choice spot
For insane princes,
Your son, cozening the red-haired heretic bastard
Who never felt a babe at breast
Nor knew a man between those strategic Tudor thighs:
Were the tears shed by you, Queen of Hearts, Widow,
For the lack of aces up your velvet sleeve?
And when the knaves Cecil and Walsingham
Played that fool Babbington as trump,
Were you so very much surprised to learn, Madam,
That Boleyn's daughter had marked your card.
Presenting you with that final bill, saying,
Off with her head?
And when the bright axe fell on you, princess,
I read how it revealed your bright deceiving wig,
Allowing the farthingaled bitch to make allusion
To alopecia: as a modern woman
Full of rageous empathy, I know
That this was the unkindest cut of all
And so none of it was really worth it,
In the end.

A Change of Direction

Our fling was flung
Our thing was done
It was not as 'twas wont to be:
Instead of flair when we were bare
He lay inert, dead beneath the duvet.
I tried suspenders, wore a snorkel,
Used the washing up gloves, faute de mieux;
Got up gum-bootily I smote him bodily
With crisp bags;
Once, I burst out of the wardrobe stark
Apart from a stethoscope and rope
Shouting Surprise! Surprise!
He sighed. Said he had an early rise ahead
And would I kindly
Go to bed?

'How's Fred,' I said next day at dinner, 'my dear?'
Getting his gaze up off his goujons, he coughed,
'He's fine,' then ceased, his brow creased
With indigestion, or deep thought:
'Got himself a new bird, Mandy.
Seems she growls when she feels randy.'
He frowned but I inferred he found it stirring
So clutching his straws come bed-time,
I started purring.

He failed to comment, apart to ask
After my sinuses and showed me
His Vick-Stick.

The next time during carnals I tried to howl
But gave a yowl. He said 'Cucumbers?'
Then made a suggestion

Of a bi-carbonate nature.
Striving for the sinuous, I hissed
But instead of reptile, I sounded febrile.
That was Monday, Tuesday I whined, Wednesday
I rested.
Thursday I honked, hooted, cooed and mooed
But he remained unmoved.
Friday after lights out, I tweeted in his ear:
Aroused, he went downstairs, hunting for budgies.
The weekend came. Saturday I screeched, I mewed, I
                                        yapped
While we flapped about,
I grunted neighed and roared
And hoped that he adored
Just one of them . . .
Was he deaf? Yes, so Sunday, desperate,
I did what giraffes do.

At last he spoke: 'When are you due
For God's sake? I can't stand anymore
Of your PMT's, my mother never had 'em, it's a bore,
It's driving me mad, I've had it with you
And my week in the zoo!
The noise! The din! I can't concentrate
It's all part of a plot to emasculate me!'

'Oh really? What about Mandy, growling in bed?
Don't you want to be on a par with Fred?'
'Fred?'
'Fred!'
'He's nearly dead from stress'.
She's the cat, but he's the mouse,
Makes him crawl nude, squeaking, around the house
On his knees! If he's good; she gives him cheese!
He's in a trap, poor chap, like me.

This last week's been hell: fear, dear,
Has had me in its grip.
Your repertoire is giving me jip,
A quiet night and a kip is all *I* crave – '

So I went to bed, as silent as the grave.
I yipped not, neither did I yowl
Nor brayed nor barked nor imitated fowl.
I spoke not: not one word nor vowel
Consonant with my position
Escaped my lips.
I was mute.
The brute complained.

'Cat got your tongue? Unbung your gob
So when you're bare I'll know you're there.
Make sweet moan, grunt, groan or sob:
You're like a sack of King Edwards
When I'm on the job!'

                    The slob!

So I went round to Mandy's
Trailing a tail and two pink ears
And I stood before her and auditioned in tears.
And she opened quite wide her green cat's eyes
As Fred slunk out and I skipped inside
And It's a gay day, dears, I think you'll agree
When it's cream for the pussy
And Brie for me.

(Eeeeeeeeeeeeeeeeee!)

Try and Get Upstairs First

Rolling on carpets is bad
For shirts:
The strain of the pounding heart
Bursts the bounds of buttons
And ping
Off they come, along with socks
Shoes, shorts. Jewellery
Takes longer.
Earrings
Hook into sweaters
And distort. Watches are in particular
Danger.
Trousers pick up cat hairs
Dresses crumple. So what?
It only cost a fortune.
Drag it off and hurl it on a chair.
Slowly a circle of debris accumulates
In a crumple of male-female fabrics,
Not much left now. Try and ensure
That both his socks
Are off:
It can cause distraction if noticed.
Put the cat out.
Do not be caught, being watched
By Tommy, paws folded under
Inscrutably
Having a look.
As your head comes down to the floor

Refrain
From commenting on the dust you find
Beneath places you don't usually look beneath.
Tomorrow is Sunday and you can have a good hoover then.

Involuntary moaning may take place,
Especially if he bangs his head on the grate.
To cover unwarranted sounds
Causing offence
Let the neighbours see you
Sucking on an asthma pump, tomorrow,
In the front garden.
You may find all sorts of things
Beneath the sofa cushions
As you claw at them for support.
Those things which were lost
May be found
But rejoicing should be low-key
Unless it's a one pound coin.
It's too late now to draw the curtains,
You can't stop now
But keep at least your head
Down
Otherwise an ambulance may arrive,
A kindly voyeur convinced of heart attack.
Imagine explaining this particular
Kiss of life.
It is inexplicable
Unless
You claim short sight.
Meanwhile, pay attention
To what you are doing.
Forget that you left the door open
And a draught is now catching you
On the upsurge.
Afterwards, if you're concerned
About the effects
Of primal juices on the Wilton
Casually clear up
With a handful of your Janet Reger
It saves getting a cloth from the kitchen.

85

Oh.
One more thing.
As you walk down the hall without benefit of cladding,
Remember that the porch door
Is made of glass
And people who live in such houses
Shouldn't.

First published *Cosmopolitan*, March 1987.

Frère Phèdre

J'ai appris lire le français classique
Sans savoir parler frog chic.
Vous voulez savoir
D'où vient mon prédicament
Et pourquoi il y va de ma gloire?

Prenons par caprice le mot 'dentifrice'.
Racine n'a pas eu de dentifrice
Parce que Racine n'a pas eu longtemps
De dents.

The Bulldog Breed

They wanted kids but weren't quite sure
How to start. It was hit or miss. He aspired to kiss her:
Not knowing you were expected to respire,
She held her breath.
He prolonged the embrace, becoming expert.
She went unconscious, becoming inert.

Out of hospital, they tried again.
He read *The Joy Of Sex*, then touched her breast.
His zest earned him a broken arm and leg,
A victim of women's defence-class reflex.
Vexed, she thought he was after her bus pass
And left him nearly crippled on the grass.

He came out in bandages but he loved her still
So with a will, he tried again
And offered up his manhood for a random tickle,
Unfortunately, as she began to nibble, lockjaw struck.
                                              Clamped
They cycled circuitously to the surgery
On his tandem.

The doctor had to break her chin
Before they could again begin.
This time, thigh-high, involuntary spasm
Led, not to orgasm, but a leggy scissors chop
That broke his nose. He reared up, bleeding
Fell down, and crushed her toes.

But they were British: what they'd started
They had to finish
Or die in the attempt.
Sadly, at the rematch she managed to catch

Her long blonde hair in his zip. Scared but strong
She panicked, tipped him over and was scalped.

Healing, her hair appealing in a crew-cut
They gave in to lust: this time
It was baby or bust, so they went for it.
Alas! He aimed too high, thrust,
Missed and poked her in the eye
Obliterating vision.

Which was unfair – it was his turn for injury.
                                    Black-patched
And unable to see what she was looking at,
She gamely grabbed a snatch in the general area
Of his lap, causing it to snap in two.
He had it splinted, good as new.

Stoked, suffused, they felt confused.
Patched and plastered, black and blue,
They had to master the technique
Or their hopes of progeny were bleak.
Grazed by defeat, they took one more risk:
This time, together, they slipped a disc.

Remember, though, their genes: members
Of the Island Race, true blue through and through,
They lay in separate hospital beds
And faced the facts. Happily, they found the means
To procreate without these scenes of injury or stress:
In due course as it came to pass they had their family in a
                                                        glass,

For, *In Vitro Veritas.*

Re-Write

Mr Darcy: Not love at first sight, Ms Bennet
But 'in the end',
Reluctantly almost,
Carefully cautiously
In spite of
Not wanting to daring to hoping to
Like
Someone
Like you,
Making allowances –
Your accent, your family. Your Mother! No
Romance;
I'm not asking you for the gusto of god-like
beings
Who anyway ended up
Messily,
Asps, you know, or drowning
In dire straits.
Or as a result of some far-fetched fooling
With philtres,
All death and daggers
In a tomb –
Not asking for this at all
But ready to accept something
More worn, cracked, like an honourable
Old tea-pot
Still gallantly ready to pour a sterling
Cup that cheers: be my old Spode
And don't expect too much, will you?
Not even total
Fidelity
Honesty
And exclusivity in passion?

After all, we are, most of us a
Little bit unable to be
So austere, so Roman matronly or
So Cato-tonic: it's passé, its day is done.
If you fancy me now
As I fancy you, after work, twice a week,
Then it will be something chipped
With faults in it
But for all its flaws and patches
It will still be
Acceptable.
Tea-up, Elizabeth?

Ms Bennet: I drink coffee.

The Unmarried Mother

She came into the FP clinic, a bleach job
Bobbed, mini-skirted, sweet sixteen.
Bouncingly uncontraconcepted, it could be seen at a
    glance
What a credit she was
To a failed Sex Education, GCSE:
Well beyond the hope or scope
Of this establishment, gone on before
By several months,
She swayed, splay-footed by the door.

''Ello Miss,' she said, 'Remember me?
It's Rhona Phillips, ex 5C!'

The room turned as one woman
And looked at Miss,
Red-faced, down-cast, caught out.

'Taught me all I know
About God,' she said, 'Still do RE? Sin, Sodom, and so on?
Morals too. 'Ere, you're a one! Not married? Or affianced?
So what you doin' in the Family Plannin' queue?
I din' realise teachers 'ad intercourse.
Well, not your sort, not you –
No offence, but oo'd 'ave thought
That sex was up your street?'

They gripped their bags!
Would you want this woman teaching your child?
All the Laura Ashley world-wide
Could not hide her carnal intent, revealed
As she sat, Pill-crazed (or was it cap?)
Imagine, if you want, this Miss wantoning!

Books unmarked, the *Times Ed. Supp* despoiled
Upon the floor, hush puppies aloft
And barking for more . . . an outbreak of tutting,
Cutting me down to size.
One sought the source of modern rot, decay?
Then seek no further girls, for there it lay, it was her,
Revealing the low moral fibre
Of the Ealing teaching profession.

'Anyway, can't stop to chat. Just bookin' in
For the birf, an'at.
S'all their fault I'm in this state:
Winston din' rate their poll-tax-payer-pink durex:
Ses sex gotta be colour-coordinated, not just free
An' insisted on an efnic minority tint
What they din't
Fink they could do.
Still. Nice to see someone's getting a leg-over
Even if it's only you. 'Oo is it?
One of those big black prefects?
It's not that dope, the 'ead, I 'ope?'

She laughed.
They looked.
The lady came.
'Next! Hey you! Come back!' She called in vain.

I skipped round Rhona
Out
Into the rain.

And nine months later, dear, there's you and then there's
me,
For the hand that rocks the cradle's mine, love –
Thanks to Rhona Phillips, ex 5C.

Phoenix

Brought up hard in those days we were
Us girls, all vested, wearing flannel drawers
Doing duty as dusters, after: oh yes,
Many's the time I've seen my Pa
Polishing the car with old Liberty-Bodices
With which no-one took none,
Us being Chapel, the Yanks based just up the road
And not allowed to catch a glimpse or grab a feel
Of fine English flesh, fifteen, no, especially not
The contents of your Living-Bra – a living death
Restricting breath in elastic bondage
Designed to last a lifetime
Once you'd found the wherewithals to fill them;
And there was going to grammar school
Gripped in a girdle, proof against rude youth, pink
With rubber suspenders and your granny
Talking Enlightenment and hinting at worse, whalebone
And corset torture before the War.
Oh brought up hard in those days we were dear
And always locked the bathroom door
Even when we wed: experienced the throes
Of passion through floor-length winceyette
With the lights off.

For me, the Blesséd Mary (Quant, that is) came too late.
I was already trussed up in what was out of date, but Right
Although my sister, Eileen, younger, knew benefit of tights
And minis, showing all she'd got: glamorous she was,
                                        saucy.
Not like me. Anyway. One day she sent me a parcel and a
                                        note.
'Life begins at fifty-three,' she wrote, 'Put 'em on Flo!
                                        Feel Free!'

I found inside these satin camis, laced but not
To say the least, straitly, and I fell in love.
Kissing goodbye to Aertex and healthy ventilation
I gave my heart (tart) to a slip of oyster-coloured slither
A handful of frill and froth, beribboned, aware
That Mother wouldn't care for it
And the PE teacher (Hygiene and Hockey) would despair –

At home alone, kids out and George at work
I closed the bedroom door: my heart knocked
At my thermals.

Off then with the old D-cups, farewell
To my vest and best navy knickers, healthful, outdoors,
Gusseted. And then the girdle, stout armour of the goodly –

But I wanted to be badly, badly.

So, stripped like a gently blushing prawn
I put on the naughty nicks, over the top
Of lace suspenders. Stockings, seamed, next
The thigh! Oh my! The gaps, the holes, the flimmery-
                                        flammery nature
Of my flummery!
The softness: smooth, seducing: the little knotted
Rosebuds, the lacy bits you could see through!
Guess what? No? Yes! Nipples!
And worst of all, poppers, poppers in unseemly places,
The whole wide open
To infiltration!

At first I told him shyly the doctor said
I had to wear a surgical appliance – in bed.
He blenched, but bravely asked to see.

So I showed him.

Next morning, after thirty years of being wed to me
My George got up first, went down
And made the tea.

So

So,
He started coming round in June
Soon giving me dirty looks and hinting
At allergies, asthma and worst of all calumnies,
Fleas.
I ask you.

So,
When they went up, I took care
To be there, curled up and kissable on the quilt,
Purring, chockful of charm.
Took him ten minutes to get me down
Into the kitchen: tripped him bare on the stair
Jestfully – When he'd found the plasters,
She'd lost the urge.

So,
He had to start over.
She made the tea, come the morn
And I shot up and jumped on the dawn
Pillow. Posed in a roly-poly way
And squeezed out cute noises as he dozed on the bed.
Scratched his nose, leaping over his head.
She laughed.
Get it off, he said, I want to, you know,

So,
I skipped off and waited till he was in mid-stroke
Then made my come-back, as a joke.
First I crept up and just watched, out of reach.
Threw him a bit, that did, when he noticed
The basilisk stare, but he carried on
Bouncing, and I timed it, pouncing
Crucially.

Got a grip through the sheet
And gave him a four-paw
Full frontal claw treat –
A satisfactory result, I feel, ensued.
He screamed, 'That rude-word cat! I'll kill it!'
And she screamed, 'That little harmless
Creature! One of God's Innocents! How
Could you, you Brute, when Pussy only wants to play?'

So,
There they were both screaming and I was
Bouncing off the walls, screaming
Louder than both. Managed to pee
On his trousers in passing
In my terror at his bad language.

So,
After that he tried a new tack
And bought me sardines.
I was sick on his new P. Cardin track
Suit and crawled onto the duvet,
Mewing pathetically so he couldn't
Thump me. Rolled over, choked and lay there
Pretending to die, poisoned. She cried
And stroked me, I put my head
On her whatsit, so he had to take
His hand
Off. (If looks could kill.)

So,
Then he tried shutting me out
But I got in the window of his new
Volvo and ripped up the seats.
I hate red and black stripes anyway
And she said, it was raining, what did
He expect? Next, he got her a god-damn puppy,
Would you believe,

So,
I beat it up, then
Just as he was trying for a new variation
Requiring stamina and split-level
Timing, I had five kittens on the bed,
Because my timing was always
Better than his:
End of month, end of story.

Good House-Keeping

I looked as through a glass darkly
And saw a bush upon my head
Burning for a restyle.
I went to the salon down the road,
But Sandra smiled wanly, she wasn't sure:
I saw myself as rather Raphaelesque
My curls in need of treatment
To prevent their Botticellying round my face,
But Sandra said I was a Hippy, a disgrace,
And it wasn't often such were seen
Chez Sandra.

She fixed it. Sandra fixed me good.
Off it came, a yard of mousey frizz
Well treasured.
I hadn't seen my ears
For years. She bleached me white.
She gelled me up in spikes.
I couldn't get my headscarf with the horses on
And went home, tonsorially nude.
The dog barked, the cat spat, the baby
She turned blue:
He made the sign of evil advising me to sue.

I had a cry
Then got out a dusty box of tricks,
A roll-on or two, a deeply plunging dress
High-heeled, made-up, I hit Hanwell.
The checkout boy checked me out and flipped
The grocer groped my pears with feeling
And moving on, two men at a bus-stop
Tipped me as a red-hot favourite
While a grandad turned to stare

Making 'it shouldn't be allowed' noises
With his lips.
Next day as I played,
The milkman curdled the milk
Muttering 'Harlow? Monroe? Yates?'
His cream-top clotting
In his heating hand
As he passed it over the gate.

The roots growing out, I returned
Chez Sandra.
'How's it bin Blondie?' she enquired
As I came tottering in
The sins of the world on my shoulders.
I told her, about men.
How yellow hair makes them bolder, brings out the beast
That lurks 'neath cloth-cap, peak and bowler.
Even the bobby's eyes lit up like red stroke amber,
Hubby by now was sulking where first
He'd mocked: he'd promised himself an object
Of desire whom he preferred
Obscured: he locked me up.

I'd climbed out and down the drain pipe
To tell Sandra
It was all a strain.
I had the hair but not the brain
That goes with bleach.
'Oh, wig me woman!' I implored
And Sandra did.
She dug me out a brown Sandy Shaw
Fashionable circa 1964. Long, lean and lank
Hiding all, I peered forth
Through a Cleopatra fringe recherché
The usual timid bore restored,
Hirsuté.

So now we're back to normalcy
The new hairdo was making
Waves
For me: I gave it up.
I'm happily hoovering once more
A hippy housewife in a pinafore
And hair-piece: apart from that it's all the same
Except for Fridays.
That's when the milkman comes round
And has a cup of tea.
If I want it off, I take it off, he has it off
And we get our yogurt free.

The Feminine Principal

Gird yourself for the bathroom slog
Ready? Then steady go into the bubbles
And assuage the less than perfect skin,
Scrape out the pits, pummy the bum
And shave the hairy leg. Strive
For the tactile suavity
Of an egg. Prune pubes.
Apply contents of costly tubes
To face, simultaneously shampooing
The hair. Out, damned spot, then
Out. Dry. Take care
To anoint with unguents
Those bits best bared
Under a discreet wattage, later.
Quelle naturelle smell
And deodorise the thighs, rouge breasts and perfume well.
Exfoliate, emolliate and depilate
Any whisper of a whisker: you are a girl.
Blow dry the crowning glory, confirm the curl
With the unloving grip
Of the heated roller. Then
Banish blemish and foundate the face,
Shape with pink flush the cheek that never knew a blush
Kohl and eyeshadow with lush turquoise
The heavily mascaraed eyes, water-proofed
Against aesthetic weeping, in keeping with your perfect
                                                    poise.

Stick on
The lipstick. File talons, polish nails
Toes too, unless you're slack then back
To the hair. Brush.
Invest
An hour or two

In vestment, padding, pulling in, mould
And behold; a living legend
Breathes softly in the gloom
Of an unusually hushed
Green-room: She walks
In Beauty,
Divine Androgyne:
Every year, at this time of Miracles,
He becomes She, the Widow Twanky,
Ready

For Aladdin
And his hanky-panky

A Winter's Tale

When my lover stayed on winter nights
I knew he was best snared bared,
Though I couldn't afford the central heating:
I put a couple of cats down the bed to warm it,
Often neglecting to turf them out
Because fur and purr is better
Than bloody freezing.

After he'd gone, smirking in a chilly dawn,
Warm at the memory of my scanties,
I took off the sensuous wraps I'd worn
For frantic antics: dressed down in my dressing-gown
I put on candlewick and fishermen's socks
Because silk and its ilk
Is bloody freezing.

Later I would meet him down the pub.
I wore boots and French knickers in the snow
And the wind whistled round where
It didn't ought to go, turning
My nose blue. Before he got there
I'd drink three gins and turn it red (wouldn't you?)
Because I was bloody freezing.

When we went social, I wore my best polyester
Dress, dynasty-styled for bronchitis and pneumonia:
Short, with shoulder-pads wide, cut low,
My crystal earrings collected ice
Like stalactites. Sheer nylon stockings
Kept my legs nice
And bloody freezing.

After I'd been married to him sometime
The case for being bare when he was there receding,
I packed up all my flimsies in a box
And settled for hand-knit knicks, Fair Isle socks
Fingerless gloves, a brace of bras, a ski-hat, long-johns
And ear-muffs, because I'd had enough
Of being bloody freezing.

He then complained, wanting to know
How I'd got to go from sex kitten to Eskimo Nell,
Togged like an Inouit in moon-boots as well:
He said he couldn't even see,
Let alone get his nooky any more.
So I told him: get me a bigger boiler,
Or wait for the bloody thaw.

Angst

I loved you, Reggy, when first I saw you on your new racer,
Bum in the air, your tousled hair
Blowing in the wind as the school bus passed.
Amazed, struck a blow hard to the heart
I pressed my face to the steamy window
And gazed, a fat schoolgirl with curly hair
When all the world was Twiggy,
Bare of weight, boney, long locks falling
In Shrimpton tresses like girlish Shetland ponies:
I was homely, I was plain. 'You'll grow into your looks'.
In vain my mother tried to comfort me. I cried.

You scorned my love. They told me so in class.
The frumpy fifth former died a death
Each time she passed you, clear laughter
Ringing in her ears, the faces of her friends
Spiteful with adolescent malice. I wept for you, Reggy.
Stuffing a pillow in my mouth at night
To fight down the sobs so's not to rob my parents
Of their sleep. Only the dog knew. I sighed into Monty's
                                                            ear.
He wagged a lot, licked my puffy face and didn't mind
The mirrored ugliness, reflected there.
I knew I could only be a nun, after this. All I had
Was brain. The pain, Reggy, of loving you
Scarred me.

Time got me in his grip and gave a squeeze.
I passed the Oxbridge Scholarship with ease
And left you, my darling, behind.
You never saw the duck become a swan.
No longer plainer than a camel's arse, I became the new
                                                    Helèna.

I passed more exams, a professor cordon bleu, later, movie
                                                        star,
I swam the media billows far
From you and the garage you worked in,
A petrol pumping man.
The world was my oyster
And yet

In my moister moments I remembered you
Your bike, your bum, the way you used to chew
Your gum and stick it on the desk. Oh happy blob
That pressed the lips of Reggy! If only you had masticated
                                                        me
I would not now return to you, a prodigy
Driven by my passionate yearning
To find you out, clad in the trappings of my earnings.
I long to shout Hey Reg! Remember me? Recall?
It's fatty Fiona, the one you wouldn't dance with at the
                                                        Ball
Claiming I was like a sherman tank, rank
With California Poppy, soppy goofy grotty, spotty?

Snug in my mink, I sink back into the lush embrace
Of my new pink roller. Gustave gave me champagne
Then drove me to Dereham in the rain, seeking
I know not what: my youth? A chance to do it all again
And get it right?
I recalled it all, looking for a Shell garage to see
If you'd done well, checking my blonde locks in the mirror
Slicking my mouth Paloma Picasso Red,
Remembering the nights I'd spent
Weeping, teenaged, with Monty my old dog on the bed:
Dead now, of course.

And then I saw you.
You saw me.

You stood bowed by the pump, your nozzle in your hand
And gave me a look like a startled fawn
Spilling the petrol on the ground, black blood.
Oh and Reggy, I recalled the pain! My first love!
You were older now but Age could not wither you
You looked the same, except you'd lost your hair
Had never had your teeth fixed (two bad) and were bent
    low
From too much cycling, deformed, how sad!

To me it made no difference!
What did Fatty goofy grotty spotty Fiona care?
At last! Oh joy! You were there!
'Reggy?' I called your name.
You half-turned to stare – you'd lost an eye
Yet still you saw me, just
And my bust heaved with jewels and the need
For quittance.
Gustave opened wide the Rolls Royce's door
– Poor Reg! I saw your wooden leg
And old Monty's great great-grandson
Got out, pissed, and bit the other one.

You bastard.

Low Expectations

Some time has passed
Since you last
Had your knees
Up, around your ears: fears
Of discoid slip loom large so whoa girl,
Steady as she goes:

To save your spine, the doctor said, stop showing off,
Slow down in bed.
As you describe his dorsal ricking, it is, I doubt
Entirely due to digging
And horticultural fervour is not at fault.
Adding, and if it is,
Then a lot more is meant
By allotment
Than was dreamed of
In the Perfumed Garden.

Meanwhile the mind shifts and fills
With the pressing need
To get the early runners in, from seed . . .

Ooh!
Ah!

And another thing. Seeing the beans upon the plate
Enbuttered in some now lost future state,
When was the last time
He took you out
For nose-bag?
Hard to know: your down-side up: puff, pant,
Slip
Slide.

111

Tricky, this bit. Still, take pride
In virtuosity. Practice makes perfect
Like pasta freshly fried –
That's it! Two whole weeks since Gino's place!
It all comes back as face to face
You breast the crests of passion;
The earth moves and shaken, stirred,
All thoughts of tagliatelli
Are now interred.

'How was it for you babe?'
'Funny,' he says, turning tender, 'the things you think of
When you're entwined. Your disc. The doc.
But lasagna, lover, was chiefly on my mind.
I felt so hungry! The thought of pasta
Made me go
Faster
To get it over with.'

And this is why I love him so!
Two like minds, not admitting impediment
A single thought
Is all you ought
To know.

Later, filled to the gills on vongole, chianti-sluiced
Your thoughts come back to sex.
Eat, suck, slurp, moan and groan
Go home: make love imaginatively:
Talk low of growing parsnips later in the year
While he burbles Arsenal's chances tenderly
In your ear.

Fashion Victim Forty

Being a girl, callow and sallow
I rolled my hair in sausage curls
And wore puffed up skirts,
Big petticoats that scratched
And winkle pickers that provoked corns,
Bred bunions, while a tight belt
Compressed my form, forcing my bust out
Like a shelf, which all the boys
Hoped to dust.

Then came that brat Twiggy: the bent was bones.
Pneumatic bust bum and tum were honed:
I starved to look like a plank, side-on.
No bumps or lumps, just a bundle
Of ribs in Mary Quant bibs, the wind
Chafing my inner thighs as I traipsed
Thro' British climatic conditions,
Courageous in Courrèges, skinny in a mini.

The hair was wrong. Curls were dead.
I ironed it instead until it hung
Like rip-cords around my head. I was dyeing it
Black Tulip, at least in patches,
And my eyes wore black, two-tiered eye-lashes
Of finest plastic. I was hip by now,
Wore grandma's skirt, beads and a headband
Which gave me bad migraine. Peace and love, man,
Except to my Dad, who made me walk behind him
When in tow
So no-one would know
We were related.
After that, I got bell-bottomed.
My flares flew and flapped

As my wing-collars took off, me wrapped
In half an Afghan goat for a coat
Which struggled into life from time to time.
Next, a character from a Japanese kabuki,
In a droopy crochet cardi, platform-soled,
Long-booted, laced, I faced pedal panic
And digital claustrophobia daily ensued.

OK, so by now I'm getting mature,
With corns and bunions and varicose veins, chilblains,
I've been buxom or anorexic to order, amoebic in my flow
As in and out my shape it goes, up and down my heels, my
                                                          hem
According to the throes of chic, the dictates
Of Them, the little men in London, Paris, Rome
My hair's been afro-combed, straight, short, long
But always too little too late, always wrong,
Black blue red blonde spiked gelled,
No one liked it shaved, punk.
A ton of junk make-up over the years
Has given me
Cosmetic fatigue.

I've had it with fashion, some of it's so vile.
I'll give it up now, this quarter century chasing style.
I'll stick to what becomes me;
A wet-suit and a shawl, socks upon my feet,
I'll wear a balaclava to keep my hairstyle neat,
A veil sometimes, to change the mood;
That'll be weekdays:
Sundays I'll go nude.

Waffor?

Bottoms up!
All Lycra-clad the class bent down
Sweat dripped and perspiration bloomed
In the hall
As they sweated it out.
Grim-faced, aerobic, their feet big in trainers
They grunted, moving their torsos
To the pounding beat.
A harpy with leopard-skin leotards
Screamed one two one two
And picked them out by name:
They took shame, red-faced from the buttocks up
At not keeping their end up:
No time for slackers, hone and tone
Before sauna, shower and sun-bed,
Then home to Slobbo,
Who leaving the pub, eating chips,
Suggests their imperfections
And impugns their hips.
So why don't these sleek goddesses seek
Their equal during these aerobic trips?
Why not the Adonis on the weights
Rippling his nipples as his pecs pop out,
Pouting under his sweat-band as the girls bend down?
He's blind to the joy of their bouncy boobs and dancing
                                                    bums
He doesn't even glance their way
Because like the real Adonis
He'll only ever really love
His mum: the best looking boys
Are gay.

Fatal Attraction

I never want to see you again!
Every time we meet
You cause me pain
And when you're gone,
God, the emptiness begins
The longing, the greed and need
To have you to myself
Once more!

Let this be the last time!
How many times have I said
Go, and lo, as soon as I see you off,
I plunge once more into grief
Spiralling down into sweet dreams
Where you and I
Are free to unite
Unrestrained by well-meant advice!

Let them talk!
Just one more time be mine
Let my lips linger, my fingers touch:
I hunger for you:
One last embrace, one taste – ah! Burns my heart
My pulses race!

But we must part.
My Mother's warning
Flashes up before my face: Don't trifle
With the Truffles;
Look what chocolate did to me!
Face it! Fight it!
You want hips size Fifty-Three?
Oh!

I never want to see you again!
Every time we meet
You cause me pain
And when you're gone,
God, the emptiness begins
The longing, the need and greed
To have you to myself.

Way Nought?

'Wort no-wun uhnderstends, lake Yenks,
Is thee effect orve pwopah bweedin
Orn thee Tohrwee wenks.
Muhmsee end Deddee must heve clarsse
Then won ken go to a twoo-bloo ekeddemmy
To git wonse vowls stwengulated end, then parse,
For awl eksemms are there for failin,
(Sept Nenny-Beatin' end DoughMestic Bliss)
Lacwosse is weally thee ohnlee pain
But won needs it to ketch
A suittible swain.'

Aye thort it over, considwin
Thee little pigs aye know
In clovah.

More arsse then kut-glarsse
Thee Upper Eshlons plow orn
Unehware thet come thee Nayntees
Thee Markits goin to be so dem Commun
They'll be lucky to git their bloo-blood
Wated hire then thet orve a negg,
Pweefurrableh en Ehwab.
Aye mean ter say
Kounts and Pwintses are two a sou,
Sew diseddvhantage comes thee way
Orve ohnly en onwobble.
Wort won't pay
Is thee fect won's wed Noddy
With Laydee Nevair Dunn-Huntin's cussin,
Thee wonderful Woddy.

119

May eddvice is to get orn dine
To Luhndon tine
End feigned a Pearly King or Qween
Before the jeck-ess euwopeens
Scoop the lort.
Then yew will look
Aye pukkah uppah clarsse membah,
Meanin, eppsolute twort.

Spite

When we first met, you didn't seem to mind
How big it was
Everything else was fine;
Smooth, pale and shapely my figure
My eyes divine with blue laguna tints
In which you claimed to rinse your soul.

Ah! The frolics of those heady days!
Dawns rosy with juvenile attraction,
The sheer vigour of our loving ways
Was enough to land other folk in traction
And you never said, then,
How big it was.

After we were wed some time
The gloss gone off,
Then you seemed to find fault
With to what you had been blind before. Love was doomed
Clouds gathered on our horizons
And you actually said how big it was.

Oh cruel the jibes! You taunted me
In front of friends
Me haunted, looking in mirrors from all angles
In despair and cursing genes.
I felt mean towards my parents
Whose fault it was how big it was.

You went right off me, comparing
Mine to yours at night, snorkelling
Through a dream-world of snores: nostrils flaring
Nose hair fluttering like gnats' legs in a breeze
And a sneeze going right off the Richter scale because
That's how big it was.

So I had a nose job, had my hooter hacked
Cut, shorn and bobbed.
How petite it was, cuter,
I was born again, my proboscis slimmed
And you fell in love with my exquisite profile, trimmed:
That's how pruned it was.

Now you're a man of many parts
Some ludicrous and most of them small
And you should have loved me ugly if you ever loved me at
                                                           all:
Before my operation I was tolerant, I was kind
I didn't really notice how hard it was to find your willy –
How silly it was!

            But now I do
            And as far as I know,
            There's no hope of corrective surgery, NHS
            For you.

Passion Killer

I was put off by the pill.
Jim didn't like his antenna
Swathed: said it transmitted static,
Long Wave. Erratic frequency
Led not to piquancy,
So for the retention
Of alternative contraception
I asked a missionary
For advice. He was nice.
'Keep your clothes on
Or wear hockey pads:
They're good for hernias, his,
In getting them off. Sluice
The erogenous zones with Jeyes Fluid.
One quick lick of this juice
Delivers him puce
While prone.
No hang-gliding. Get off the chandelier
When he is near and open the door
To admit the chill-factor.
You can then turn blue and hence frigid
While he goes rigid.
When you peer at his flower,
Sneer. No pet names, calling it Fred;
This oft leads to putting petal to the metal,
Cohabitation, then fermentation taking place
On the bed.
No aphrodisiac, liquid or mastic.
Give him blancmange. If it moves
You won't have to.
Make it pink and drink
Tap water, nitrate nourished
So his intent drops off

123

Or is bent.

If all this fails,
Put down your book.
One look at your face
Will lead to deflation.'

This worked on Jim –
But for me and the missionary
It was the start
Of the birth of a nation.

Friday Night Fever

The eternal flame burns up
Catching us wild, young and free.
You and me, babe,
Burning darling, stoking the fire,
Twisting in insane arcs of desire
To consume subsume
Each the other's
Delirium
Comes again: hot.

Touch me, crush me to you,
Never free me
From this heat in our cold land.
In a mean-streeted poorly-heated time
Save me baby so in this night we'll shine
Burning, hopeful and young
Like the great white light, pulsar
Delirium
Comes again: hot.

We'll keep on to larva flow,
Ineffable pair on volcanic regulo
Until Celsius two become one,
An element bonding in stable relations:
Scientifically we're heading for carbonisation.
Me and you and vindaloo, macerated by Madras
We'll soon fall into ash
As delirium
Comes again: hot.

Scum

I'm a manageress at work
And at home too,
Cooking washing and ironing
Sewing, gardening, dusting for you
Putting rubber gloves on to clean the loo,
You're a Man who cannot for himself
Do. My career is clear:
You're a woman's work my dear.

I make the breakfast and then the bed,
With one hand matching your socks
While with the other, I hoover your dogs.
Somehow you're always out first.
A VIP ahead of me who hogs
The car.
I'm free to take the bus
And go off worrying if you'll always be mine.
Am I pretty enough? What'll I get you for supper?
You swine.

It was the over-time led to a re-think,
I came back late, embattled, tired,
To find you, flexi-timed fresh and just bathed,
Lying laughing by the fire,
Offering drink.
You were bare to the skin
Under thin terry-towelling
Deodorised by me.

So what was new?
No thing.
Sighing, I then went to the loo
And found the bath *freshly* cleaned.

So I knew
It hadn't been
By you.

Riposte

Dear Gloria,
    I've just got back from the team's trip
    To Wapping and quite frankly, now I'm hopping
    Mad. Just a note is all you wrote, sad,
    Considering our time together wasn't all bad
    Or your memory misgives

I mean, how come you got gross so quick?
Slender as a tender dream girl, you were slick
And svelte. You felt scorn for fat folk over twenty-nine
But when you hit thirty, oh baby, you became porcine,
A fat and greedy pig.

It's hormonal, you said, lolloping like a
Michelin-advert on the bed.
I slept on the edge because your bum and tum spread
So much. Wedged, I turned sportive, anything to get
                      away
From the hard sight of your hard troughing all day
A sack of wifely lard.

If I tried to stop you shovelling it in you cried
And gave me Man's historic inhumanity to wide
Women. What about me, suffering cardiac arrest
Every time you felt randy and removed your vest,
Purposefully?

What's more, what happened to the dainty half-bare
Lingerie, the frilly underwear? Did you think I
                        wouldn't care
If you went thermal, wearing socks in bed? Good thing
                  this bloke's half-blind.

129

Don't let him get contact lenses. He'll find he needs more
Than assisted vision
To take in your behind.

Well, fatso, I wish you joy with your pervert
And his gateaux. What will you do, revert to type
Licking chocolate and cream off his bald spots at night?
Oh, and by the way, while we're on that theme, it was
                                                    not
Wanda Wednesdays, it was Willie.

Gin's stopped play, has it dear?
Well, now you're not here
I have to say
I'm glad to be gay

So, so long,

        Your loving husband,

                John.